S0-AHR-536

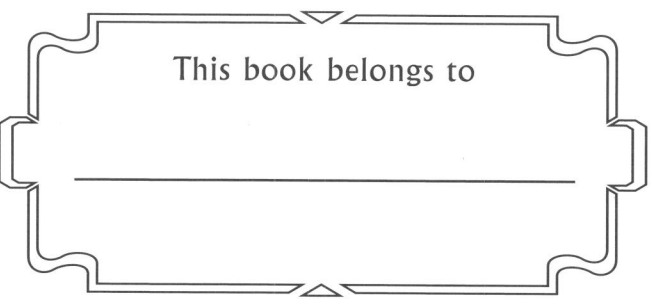

This book belongs to

_____

CHARACTERS
Buffalo Biff - Clay Smith
Ruby - Abigayle Horrell
Pete - Cody Waggoner
Announcer - Joe Loesch

Produced by: Joe Loesch
Executive Producer: Cheryl J. Hutchinson
Developed and Created by: Toy Box Productions
Story Written and Recorded by: Joe Loesch
for **Creative License, Inc.**
Art Direction and Character Illustrations by:
Brian T. Cox, **for Toy Box Productions**

Manufactured exclusively by
CRT, Custom Products, Inc.
℗ © 2003 Toy Box Productions,
A division of CRT, Custom Products, Inc.
7532 Hickory Hills Court,
Whites Creek, TN 37189

1-800-750-1511   www.crttoybox.com

ISBN 978-1-932332-21-6

21 sq.ft twin movable vertical rear rudders

1903 Wright Flyer

6.2 foot seperation

21.1 foot overall length

510 sq foot area

Rt. wing 4 inches longer to compensate for extra weight of engine

Meet the Wright Brothers

Welcome to another adventure with our time travelers.
Who hasn't dreamed of flying? Wilbur and Orville Wright did.
Since Orville Wright took his first flight on December 17th, 1903,
our world has never been the same.

Let's see what our Raiders have in store for us.

We're on our way to meet the Wright brothers.

Prepare for another blast into the past with
Buffalo Biff and Farley's Raiders!

1/20 camber

48 sq. ft. double horizontal front rudder

40.3 foot span

0.83 foot anhedral

6.5 foot chord

605 Lbs.

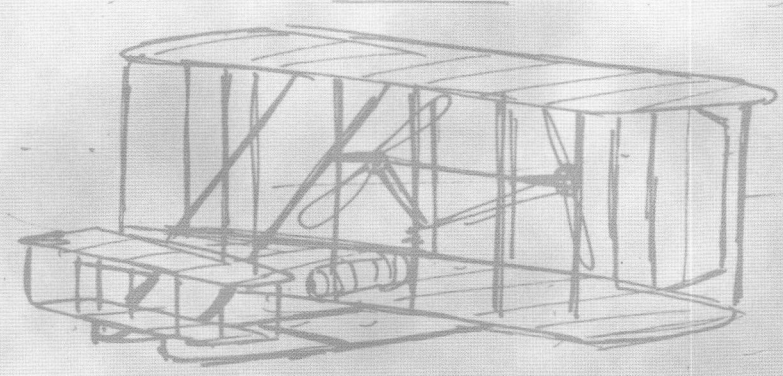

Dreaming OF Flying

Ruby: What in the world is wrong with that boy, Biff?

Biff: He's day dreaming, Ruby. Haven't you ever wondered what it would be like if you could fly?

Ruby: Well, I suppose I have.

Biff: When I was little, I used to run down that very hill and imagine that I would take off into the wild blue yonder at any moment! The feeling was overwhelming.

Ruby: Yes, I remember that feeling! I still get that feeling every time we take off on another adventure in the time machine!

Biff: Exactly!

Pete: That was great! I imagined I could fly, and there for a moment I thought I was!

Ruby: Imagination is a wonderful thing.

Biff: Imagine what it would be like today if the Wright Brothers had never dreamed of flying.

Pete: If they hadn't taken that first flight someone else would have.

Biff: That's true. But, thank goodness, they followed their dreams. I used many of their principles in designing our time machine.

Ruby:	Like what principles, Biff?
Pete:	Yes, like what principles, Biff?
Ruby:	Is there an echo in here?
Pete:	Is there an echo in here?
Ruby:	Pete!
Biff:	Relax, Ruby. He wouldn't tease you if he didn't like you.
Pete:	Biff.

Ruby: Let me repeat my question. Like what principles, Biff?

Biff: Well, for example, their 'bicycle balance' and 'wind tunnel experiments'. Not to mention that they were the first to design their propellers as a form of aerofoil.

Pete: Whoa, that's a lot of information, Biff.

Biff: I guess the easiest way to explain it would be to show you.

Ruby: Oh boy, we're on our way to meet the Wright Brothers!

Biff: Gather together whatever you'll need for the trip and we'll meet in my lab first thing in the morning.

Pete: This is going to be great!

Clothes Make The Man

Biff: Good morning, Raiders.

Ruby: Good morning, Biff.

Pete: Morning!

Ruby: Here are your clothes for the time period, Pete. Biff and I are already wearing ours.

Pete: Oh, Ruby, do I have to?

Biff: You know the plan, Pete. If something should happen where we would have to leave the time machine...

Ruby: We would look pretty silly walking around in the clothes we wear today. And besides, it took me hours to make these, so put them on, please.

Pete: Oh, all right.

Biff: Pete, after you get dressed, go ahead and make your rounds. Here's the time machine checklist.

Pete: Roger that, Captain.

Biff: Ruby, please hand me that wrench.

Ruby: Here you go, Biff.

Biff: I think that just about covers everything.

Ruby: You know, dozens of people were working to invent the airplane around the turn of the twentieth century.

Biff: Sounds like you've been doing your homework, Ruby.

Ruby: Maybe just a little.

Biff: Actually, the period of active experimentation began in 1891 when German engineer, Otto Lilienthal, began experimenting with hang gliders.

Pete: Hang gliders! Hang gliders are so cool!

13

Ruby: Pete, you look adorable!

Pete: Ruby. All systems are a go, Biff!

Biff: About a hundred years earlier, Sir George Cayley realized that the lift and thrust function of bird wings could be imitated on a fixed wing aircraft.

Ruby: A hundred years earlier? That information should have given Otto Lilienthal a huge jump on the Wright Brothers.

Biff: But Otto focused his work on a fixed wing glider rather than on a complete airplane.

Pete: During this time period, people thought that those who worked on aircrafts were out of their minds!

Ruby: That's exactly right, Pete.

Biff: But once a hardheaded German engineer entered the game...

Pete: Like Otto Lilienthal?

Ruby: Right, Pete.

Biff: Other respectable people soon followed.

Pete: Like the Wright Brothers!

Ruby: I can't wait to meet the Wright Brothers!

Biff: Our Biffometer is set for Dayton, Ohio, in the year 1901.

Ruby: But their successful flight was in 1903.

Pete: And, I don't think they flew their plane in Dayton, Ohio!

Biff: That's right, but we'll want to see the exciting experiments that lead up to that momentous occasion. So, we'll first visit the Wrights in their bicycle shop.

Pete: Bicycle shop? What happened to the hang gliders?

Biff: Just be patient, Pete.

Ruby: We're about to blast off!

Biff: Hold on everyone. Here come Buffalo Biff and Farley's Raiders!

All: Yahoo!

A Flying Start

Biff: I'll slow the machine down a little so we can view the Wright Brothers conducting a flight experiment.

Ruby: Our Biffometer says we're in the year 1900!

Pete: Look, it's a glider! Hey, they're flying! I thought they didn't make their first flight until 1903?

Biff: Otto Lilienthal and others like him were flying fixed-wing gliders years before.

Ruby: But, it's the Wright Brothers who will make the first powered flight in 1903.

Biff: They referred to their glider as a 'heavier-than-air' craft.

Pete: 'Heavier-than-air' craft. Very interesting.

Those Crazy Bicycles

Biff: Here we are! Dayton, Ohio, 1901.

Ruby: Oh, I just love this time period... the clothes, the ladies hats, the architecture!

Pete: Forget that stuff! Look at those crazy bicycles!

Biff: Those were the first two wheeled cycles to be called bicycles. They were more commonly called high-wheelers.

Ruby: They were invented in 1871, and were fairly popular during the 1880s.

Pete: High-wheelers. How did we get to the subject of bicycles?

Biff: It's only appropriate since the Wright Brothers owned a bicycle shop.

Ruby: And they used their equipment to build their flying machines and experiments.

Pete: The times were certainly different back then. Or should I say back now. Say, do you suppose I could ride one of those bicycles?

Biff: Forget it, Pete, we're not getting out of the time machine.

Pete: Biff, we have these nifty turn of the century clothes that Ruby made for us. We wouldn't look out of place.

Biff: Something bad always happens when we leave our craft, Pete. Please, get this notion out of your head.

Ruby: There's the Wright Brothers' bicycle shop!

Biff: And there's Orville Wright, riding down the street on a bicycle!

Pete: That bicycle appears to be just as strange as one of those high wheelers.

Biff: That's because the Wrights added an experiment on the front of it.

Ruby: This has to be their bicycle balance experiment!

Pete: What does a bicycle have to do with flying machines?

Biff: At the end of 1901, the Wright Brothers were frustrated by the flights of their 1900 and 1901 gliders. The aircrafts were flown up to three hundred feet in a single glide.

Ruby: While they were successful in getting them off the ground, they had no control of them while in the air.

Pete: Oh, so they had to come up with a way to steer the aircraft!

Biff: Right, Pete. During the fall of 1901, the brothers began to question the aerodynamic data upon which they were basing their designs. They thought perhaps their lift and drag equations might be off a bit.

Pete: Whoa, hold on there. What are you talking about?

Ruby: Lift and drag, Pete. Lift means to raise from a lower to higher position.

Pete: Like when an airplane takes off from the ground to the air?

Biff: Right! And drag, according to the dictionary, means something that hinders progress. You know, to slow down.

Pete: So it's sort of the opposite of lift?

Ruby: Right, Pete!

Pete: But why would you want to fight against the lift?

Biff: Don't look at it as a fight, rather as... balance. Between the two, you can control the right amount of lift and the right amount of drag.

Ruby: Like a soft landing verses a hard landing.

Biff: If a wing dips on one side of your aircraft, drag can bring the aircraft back in balance.

Pete: And that's what the bicycle balance experiment is all about.

Ruby: Very good, Pete.

Pete: Very interesting! For a moment there, I thought this was going to be boring. But what about their wind tunnel experiment?

Just Blowing Through

Biff: Here we are in the bicycle shop. As you can see they took a long wooden box and forced a steady stream of air through it with a gasoline powered fan.

Ruby: Through their miniature wind tunnel experiments they could further explore their theories of lift and drag.

Biff: By producing a controlled stream of air, they could study the effects of the craft's movement on their aircraft models.

Ruby: Biff, where's Pete?

Biff: Pete! Oh, no! I can only guess where he is! Hold on, Ruby!

Ruby: He's riding a bicycle, isn't he?

Biff: There he is!

Ruby: He's on one of those high-wheelers!

Biff: He looks a little wobbly!

Ruby: A little? He's a lot wobbly! Stay on him, Biff!

Biff: I'm on him, Ruby! He turned down that alley! I don't think he knew how hard it would be to ride one of those high-wheelers!

Ruby: Now he's even more wobbly! Be careful Pete! Brakes! Brakes! Brakes!

Biff:	Ouch! He went right over the handle bars and into those trash cans!
Ruby:	If he had to go for a bicycle ride, why did he have to ride on one that was so hard to handle?
Pete:	Oh...what happened?
Biff:	You went against my orders.
Ruby:	As usual.
Biff:	You hurt yourself.
Ruby:	As usual.
Biff:	And here we are once again, out of our craft and exposed to being discovered.
Pete:	Don't say it.
Biff & Ruby:	As usual!

Ruby: Come on, Pete, let me help you up. You tore your pants!

Pete: Sorry, Ruby.

Ruby: I can fix the pants, Pete. Are you alright?

Pete: I scrapped my knee a bit, but I guess it could be a lot worse.

Biff: A lot worse! Maybe next time you'll listen to me.

Pete: Okay, okay, I get the picture. Next time I'll listen.

Biff: You've said that before.

Ruby: As usual.

All: Chuckle.

Pete: Biff, when are we going to see them fly?

Biff: Okay, Pete, I guess it's time. Hold on Raiders, we're off to see the Wright Brothers' first flight!

Next Stop, Kitty Hawk

Pete: Here we are! The biffometer reads December 17, 1903.

Ruby: We're just off the coast of North Carolina. I can see Kitty Hawk from here.

Biff: The birthplace of aviation. The Wright flight took place here, on Kill Devil Hill, just four miles south of Kitty Hawk.

Pete: Kitty Hawk looks like a quiet little fishing village.

Biff: That's exactly what it is, Pete. The Wrights wanted to find a private place to conduct their experiments.

Ruby: Looks like they found it, Biff.

Biff: The sand on the beach will allow for soft landings.

Pete: In case they used too much drag, right, Biff?

Biff: I think you've got the hang of this, Pete.

Ruby: And the ocean breezes will assist them in their flights as well.

Biff: Right! Let's move in closer for the big flight.

45

Ruby: This is so exciting!

Biff: They're about to break the bond of earth for the first time in their 'heavier-than-air' flying machine!

Pete: I can't believe we're here to see the first powered flight of the Wright Brothers!

Biff: The Wrights needed a lightweight gas engine to power their craft.

Ruby: Gas-powered engines were quite heavy at this time.

Biff: So they built their own with the help of a friend, Charles Taylor.

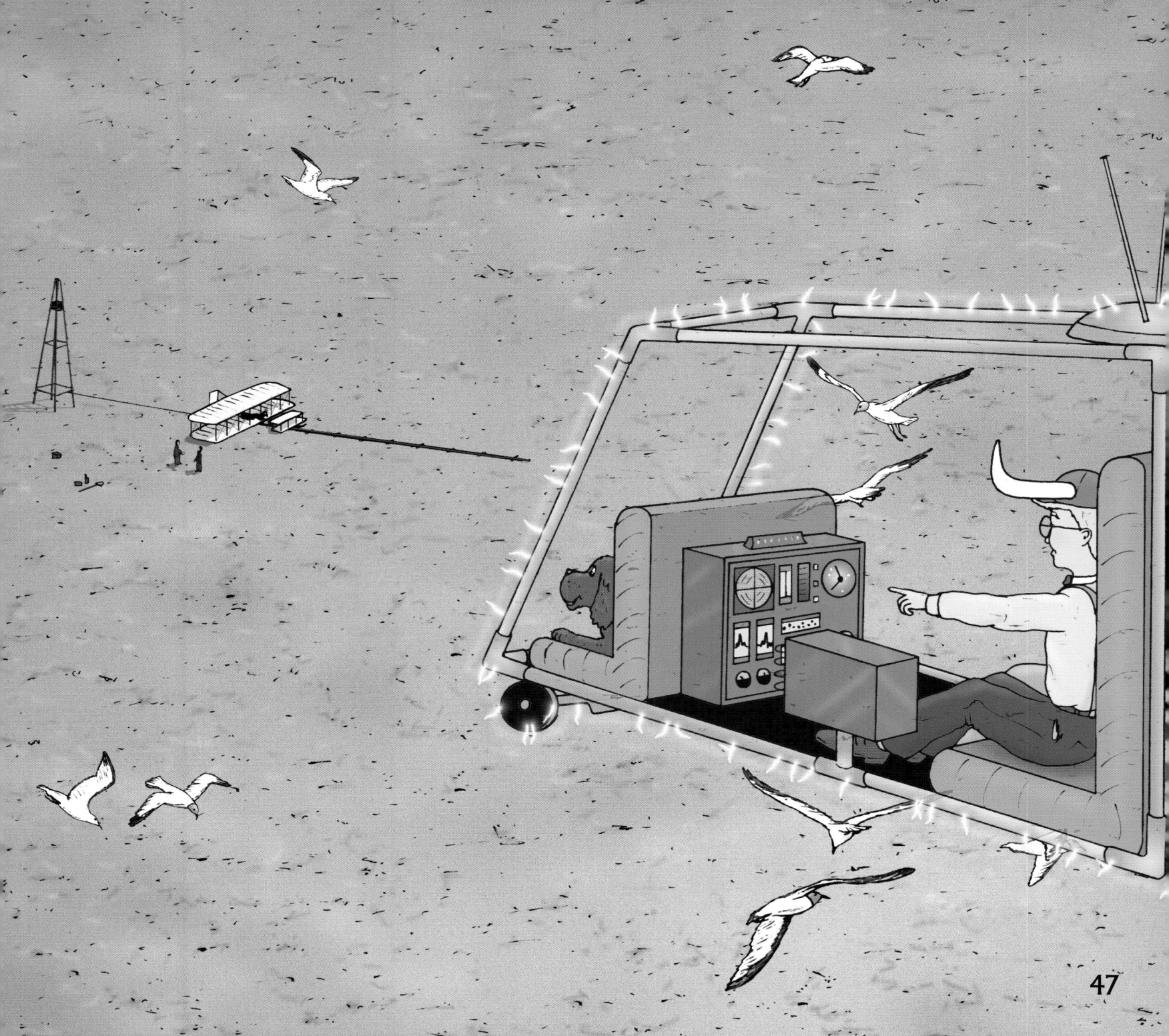

Pete: Look, the Wright Flyer is on the monorail track ready for take off!

Ruby: Their gas engine is cranked up and ready to go!

Biff: Today, Orville is at the controls. Wilbur attempted to get the flyer airborne just a few days ago.

Ruby: But things did not go well, and some repairs had to be made.

Pete: Today the weather is just right!

Biff: There they go! The flyer makes its way down the track!

Ruby: Gaining speed as it goes!

Pete: Wilbur runs beside the flyer to steady the right wing!

Biff: And, voila, the Wright flyer lifts off the monorail.

Pete: We have lift!

Ruby: How exciting! I can't believe it! Here we are experiencing this great moment of the twentieth century!

Biff: The first flight only lasted twelve seconds, and flew only one hundred twenty feet.

Ruby: It was the first controlled, sustained flight in a 'heavier-than-air' craft.

Pete: The brothers flew three more times that day.

Biff: Each time becoming more comfortable with the craft.

Ruby: Each of the brothers traveled about two hundred feet in their next two flights on that very day.

Biff: One of those flights carried Wilbur Wright two hundred feet in just fifty-nine seconds! Hold on Raiders, we're headed for home!

Pete: I'm ready to go home, Biff. I'm hungry!

Ruby: As usual.

All: Yahoo!

21 sq.ft twin movable vertical rear rudders

1903 Wright Flyer

6.2 foot seperation

21.1 foot overall length

510 sq foot area

Rt. wing 4 inches longer to compensate for extra weight of engine

Thank you for joining us for this Time Traveler Adventure.

Continue on to one of the next versions of this adventure

to become the character of your choice.

Have fun as one of Farley's Raiders!

1/20 camber

48 sq. ft.
double horizontal
front rudder

40.3 foot span

0.83 foot anhedral

6.5 foot chord

605 lbs.

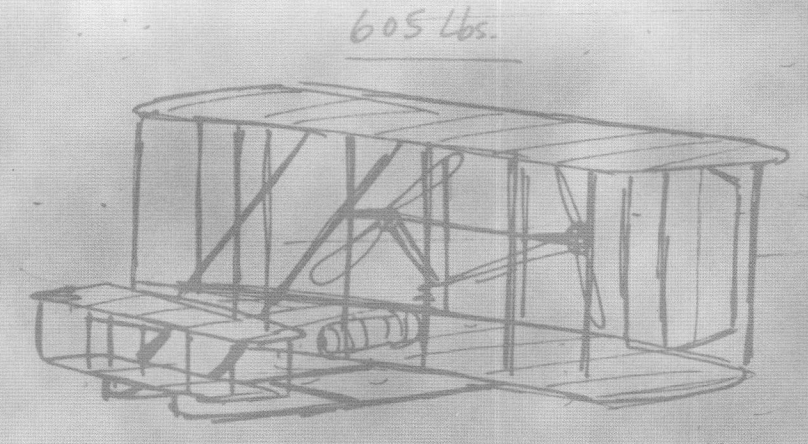